Making The (Right) Connections

A Cautionary

Account

Of WMD

Intelligence

CHARLES TUTEN

Information acquired through November 2008
used in the preparation of this monograph

ISBN print   978 1 881625 22 3 (1 881625 22 2)
ISBN digital 978 1 881625 24 7 (1 881625 24 9)

Cold War events involving intelligence on long-range nuclear missiles impart caveats fo historians and policy analysts evaluating contemporary WMD issues.

Contention regarding the role of national security intelligence in promoting the US expedition against Iraq has exposed aspects of a usually hidden process. Public, media, and academic awareness of the practical workings of intelligence analysis is essential for assessing significant policy decisions supposedly based on solid intelligence evidence. Basic to the analytic process is the collection of fragmentary information from widely varied sources, and arrangement in coherent patterns—relating not only specific evidence but also time (history), place, and concept. Intelligence failures take place when all elements of this multifaceted synthesis are not, accurately, linked. Specialized knowledge is essential, but not accompanied by blinkers that obscure alternatives and parallels. There is an omnipresent risk of misconnection, especially when subject to external direction.

The WMD (weapons of mass destruction—nuclear, chemical, biological) letterset has trickled out from the intelligence sector to become an accepted buzzword, and, along with ballistic missile delivery means, issues of wide current interest. A case study involving these issues affords the opportunity to examine intelligence at work, illustrating realities of inquiry, the convolutions and uncertainties, the known, the missed, the forgotten. Key Cold War events can now be detailed with an insider perspective, exploiting recent declassification of source material.

European media in early 2000 revealed that German historian Matthias Uhl had found evidence in Russian archives of an, apparently, unknown episode of the Cold War: the Soviet 1959 basing of medium-range ballistic missiles at two locations in the defunct German Democratic Republic. Prior supposition had been that Premier Nikita S. Khrushchev's 1962 Cub venture represented the first, and only, deployment these strategic systems outside of the USSR. T revelation attracted scant US attention. The diffu nature of information in our times is indicated by t unnoticed 1996 disclosure by a Russian missile forc general of the MRBM forward deployment in a milita journal article. Lapses in awareness of releva evidence are not unique to the intelligence arena.

Undetected transfer of MRBM into a region accessib to intense and systematic Western intelligen monitoring may have directly bolstered Khrushche confidence in similar success for a bolder move rockets into Cuba. A perceptual obverse transpired the unfortunate September 1962 US Special Nation Intelligence Estimate that cited, as the leading fact for judging that the Soviets would be unlikely to mo strategic missiles into Cuba, that these systems ha been deployed exclusively within the USSR. Th coordinated Intelligence Community assessment ha been issued 25 days before U-2 reconnaissan aircraft photographs revealed Cuban MRB equipment. In the real world, a Soviet strategic missi brigade had been externally deployed before, an likely during and after, the Cuban events. In one of t what-might-have-been highlights of the Cold Wa knowledge of the East German missiles might ha altered preconceptions of Soviet intentions, an precipitated earlier American actions that could ha changed the nature of the dangerous nucle confrontation that followed.

The 1959 MRBM deployment took place during period of heightened East-West tension involvin European missile basing and countermoves, threa real and imagined, on a stage manipulated by Sovi

The establishment on Cuban soil of a significant strike capability with such weapons would represer a sharp departure from Soviet practice, since such weapons have so far not been installed even i Satellite territory.

SNIE 85-3-62 | The Military Buildup In Cuba | 19 September 1962 opaganda. Scenes and script have striking milarities to a theater missile crisis, replayed on a rger scale, a quarter century later. Khrushchev's asts about, largely nonexistent, rockets instigated US issile moves, which in turn triggered Soviet unteraction. Events transpired similarly in the cond European missile crisis except that the Soviet reat would be very real. Two East German stallations had starring roles in both periods.

e East German basing revelation sparked the rticular interest of one former Central Intelligence gency analyst. I had retrospectively reported via assified channels in 1980 on evidence pointing to RBM deployment at the same two locations. telligence conclusions seldom receive such direct onfirmation. Presentation of my findings met with a ixed reception. Analysts who normally monitored viet military developments in Central Europe hemently rejected the MRBM conclusion. Others ecializing in strategic missiles, some working erally down the hall from the first group, mmediately recognized the evidence and accepted e basing implication. Ultimately intelligence corded a formal report the generic response to convenient findings—ignore. This essay updates and xpands that report perspective with evidence found bsequently, the German researcher's work, and ussian information. The resultant is a new inference, so awaiting validation.

definitions note: Western categorization of ballistic issiles bands the BMs by range (varying by source); a ommon arrangement has medium-range between 000 to 3000 km, with short below and intermediate r the next higher range. The Soviets defined only rategic, above 1000 km, with operational-tactical as e next lower band. English usage of (guided) missile nd (unguided) rocket contrasts with the Russian word keta, which has no such distinction. Missiles have oth Soviet and NATO designators and nicknames, ith the former having several types relating to system, ocket, range, and production. All of these terms will e used, alternating to identify viewpoints. If this

practice adds confusion, welcome to the intelligence marketplace. One of the fundamental, and all too frequent, sources of intelligence error is the superimposition, even substitution, of analysts' conceptual framework on alien environments.

Origins

Investigative teams fanning out across the territory of a defeated country. Frantically searching for nuclear, chemical, and missile vestiges, while interrogating scientists concerning technology advancement. All may seem familiar, however, this early WMD hunt began in the 1945 ruins of Nazi Germany. Had any of the extensive experience acquired, and lessons learned, been tapped for planning the post Iraq war survey? American and British specialists evinced particular interest in the German V-2 (A-4) ballistic missile that had been given a notable wartime demonstration. Across the soon-to-be Iron Curtain a parallel Soviet effort geared up. The German rocketry achievements would be the genesis of the missile programs of both sides, incorporating designs, hardware, and talent.

The British, assisted by Americans, immediately initiated Operation Backfire, assembling missiles and German V-2 crews near Cuxhaven to replicate launch procedures while personnel specialized skills remained fresh. At White Sands in New Mexico the US formed the first guided missile battalion during October. The US and Soviets soon employed German scientists and engineers for jump-starting respective enterprises. The Soviet zone encompassed the Peenemünde test center and Nordhausen factory, although American troops arrived first at the latter, stripping the underground halls of V-2 components. The Soviets initiated a rocket development effort concurrently in the eastern zone with their German assets.

In July 1946 the Soviets established their first rocket study unit near Berka, by re-designating a Ground Troops—SV (*Sukhoputnyye voyska*)—regiment as 92 Special Purpose Brigade—BON (*Brigada osobennago naznacheniya*). This trailblazing unit would evolve into an MRBM brigade that would have a major role during ensuing events. US intelligence duly noted the existence of both the Soviet effort and the new brigade, opening an order of battle entry pinpointing military unit number 57246. The assignment of unique number serials to entities at certain organization levels is a common military identification practice, and tracking by intelligence services a well-developed art. The real payoff, however, is achieved only when a number is associated with a specific entity.

Prototype missile unit 92 BON keyed exploitation of V-2 technology but no opportunity existed to conduct live firings while in East Germany. Late in 1946 the Soviets packed up their German experts and transported them into the USSR to build on their achievements in better-controlled surroundings. Soviet teams worked in parallel with German, extracting knowledge until satisfied that all useful information had been assimilated. Gradually shunted aside and isolated, the Germans would eventually be sent home. These repatriates would be important sources for Western intelligence regarding the Soviet rocket program well into the 1950s.

A May 1946 decree established the State Central Range for rocket testing at Kapustin Yar in a vast desolate region north of the Caspian Sea. In August 1947 92 BON redeployed to the range and operated as a technology test bed. A milestone achievement on 18 October 1947 involved the firing of, what the Soviets claimed as, the first native surface-to-surface rocket. Native had been loosely defined since the projectile derived from a V-2 produced with Soviet materials and labor. The BON role as a test unit continued with development of the first generation R-1 (SS-1a Scunner) and R-2 (SS-2 Sibling) SRBM. In December 1950 the rocket unit designation altered to 22 BON RVGK, joined at Kapustin Yar by a new, second, rocket brigade 23 BON RVGK.

RVGK (*Rezerv verkhovnogo glavnogo komandovaniya*— Supreme High Command Reserve) labeling manifested

a unique and preeminent Soviet concept, indicative a highly centralized state directly controlling ass that could be allocated to determine import strategic outcomes. The RVGK designation not or signified critical priorities, but also presaged transiti from an experimental to an operational force. As t force grew in dimension, strategic rockets had be developed, and ICBM deployment became immine the next (Soviet) logical step at the end of the 195 would be the creation of an entirely new branch of t armed forces, the Strategic Rocket Troops—RV (*Raketnyye voyska strategicheskogo naznacheniya*) on the basis of RVGK rocket units.

The next phase in the career of 22 BON RVC occasioned relocation to Medved (southwest Novgorod) in October 1952. There the brigade key the elaboration of control, organization, support, a field procedures for the emerging rocket force, as w as training personnel in assimilating new technolo The Soviets equipped one battalion with the R-1 second battalion specialized in the R-2; while a th battalion worked on the developmental R-5 (SS Shyster). Considerably later, émigré reports wou detail for US intelligence the mission of Medved as training brigade for SV rocket-technical specialis Signals intelligence reporting identified the BC military unit number at Medved in 1954-55. The ne significant movement of this brigade, back to E Germany, would not be detected, the track lost duri a crisis period.

R-5 represented the final V-2 derivative. According Russian information, development began in Mar 1953, with initial test firings at Kapustin Yar November. Dissatisfaction with the initial resu instigated a redesigned R-5M in April 1954, basica modified with larger propellant capacity. The 1200 k range R-5M successfully passed state acceptance tri in June 1956, deploying as the initial Soviet MRB Already, in February, the R-5M had been the fi Soviet rocket to be fired with a live nuclear warhea This system would head the Soviet rocket fleet for t next three years. Soviet development efforts had

official witness: in June 1955 the US activated
radar at Diyarbakir in Turkey specifically to
onitor Kapustin Yar. Missile technical
rameters could be collected, although
fferences between original and modified Shyster
d been poorly understood. Identifying variants
original missiles would continue to be
oblematic throughout the Cold
ar, engendering heated intelligence
ontroversies.

reation of rocket units, equipped
ith the R-1 and R-2, matched the
ace of system development.
rawing on the experience and
ersonnel of 22 BON, four additional
igades had been activated by March 1953. Re-
esignating all six then as Engineer Brigades RVGK,
ith 22 BON renumbered to 72, the "Engineer"
beling served as a cover, an attempt to conceal the
ature of a highly sensitive force. The Soviets need not
ave been concerned about disclosure—rocket units
rmation proceeded unnoticed by US intelligence.
lthough extensive technical data would be acquired
onitoring range firings, other missile program facets,
ncluding production rates and launcher deployments,
ould only be conjectured. Merely a hint of the 1950s
Engineer" units would be acquired in the early 1960s,
hen Lieutenant Colonel Oleg Penkovsky turned over
oviet classified material on rocket operations.

rogress developing the R-5M, and a new generation
f SRBM, apparently motivated the Soviets to plan an
mbitious surface-to-surface rocket force deployment.
March 1955 the Communist Party Central
ommittee decreed engineer brigade bases from the
ar East to Central Europe, while the Ministry of
efense issued regulations for the SV rocket force. In a
amiliar Soviet outcome, however, rocket development
ifficulties and lagging production caused the central
lanners' scheme to misfire. A concrete result of the
ecree, indicating the scale of MR-SRBM production
nvisioned, would be the start of construction on a
etwork of eight large rocket armament arsenals.

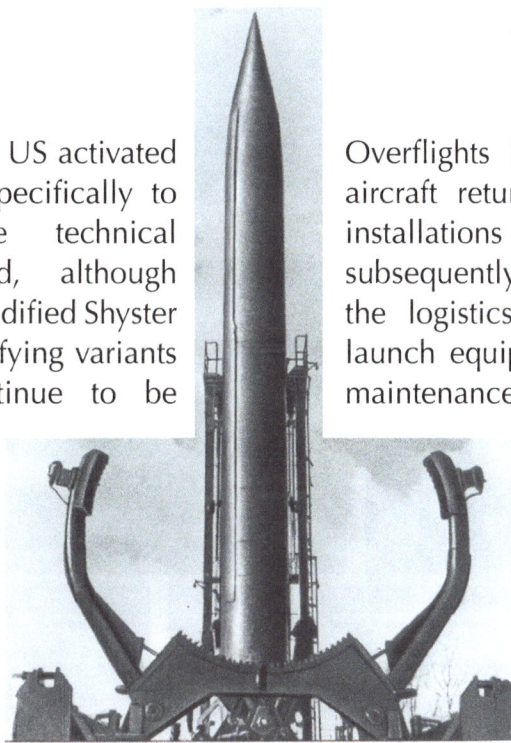

Overflights by US Genetrix balloon and U-2
aircraft returned photographs of four of these
installations during 1956 to 1958. These arsenals
subsequently transferred to the RVSN to become
the logistics hub for IC-IR-MRBM rocket and
launch equipment reserves; warhead and rocket
maintenance; systems assimilation and phaseout;
as well as operations research
centers.

Following the 1956 introduction
into service of the R-5M, existing
engineer brigades had been
rearmed so that by the end of the
year 24 launchers became available,
and the ultimate total of 48, by the
end of 1957. The brigade organization featured equipping
with a vehicular launch support complement sufficient
to support distant redeployments. A brigade had three
battalions, each of which could set up two launch
stands. Some of these brigades would eventually be
subordinated to the SV. During 1956 some individual
battalions had established permanent launch
positions. Pre-positioning had the advantages of
reducing duration of rocket launch technical
preparations, with the capability of striking targets
designated in advance. Recognition of these
advantages led at some point in 1958 to the creation
of four engineer regiments, each with two battalions,
totaling four launch stands, for permanent basing. In
the regiments, fixed support structures substituted for
the varied propellant and other vehicle types needed
in the larger, deployable, brigades. Regiments had
been based in the Western USSR at Simferopol and
Slavuta and in the Far East at Manzovka and Ussuriysk.

The rocket regiments based at permanent sites
represented the vanguard of an MRBM, and IRBM,
force that would be massively expanded in the 1960s.
Only provisory reflection of the earliest deployments
had appeared in signals intelligence, and none could
be identified on the limited photographic coverage
provided by U-2 overflights. Only from mid-1961,
with the advent of usable KH-4 (Corona) photo

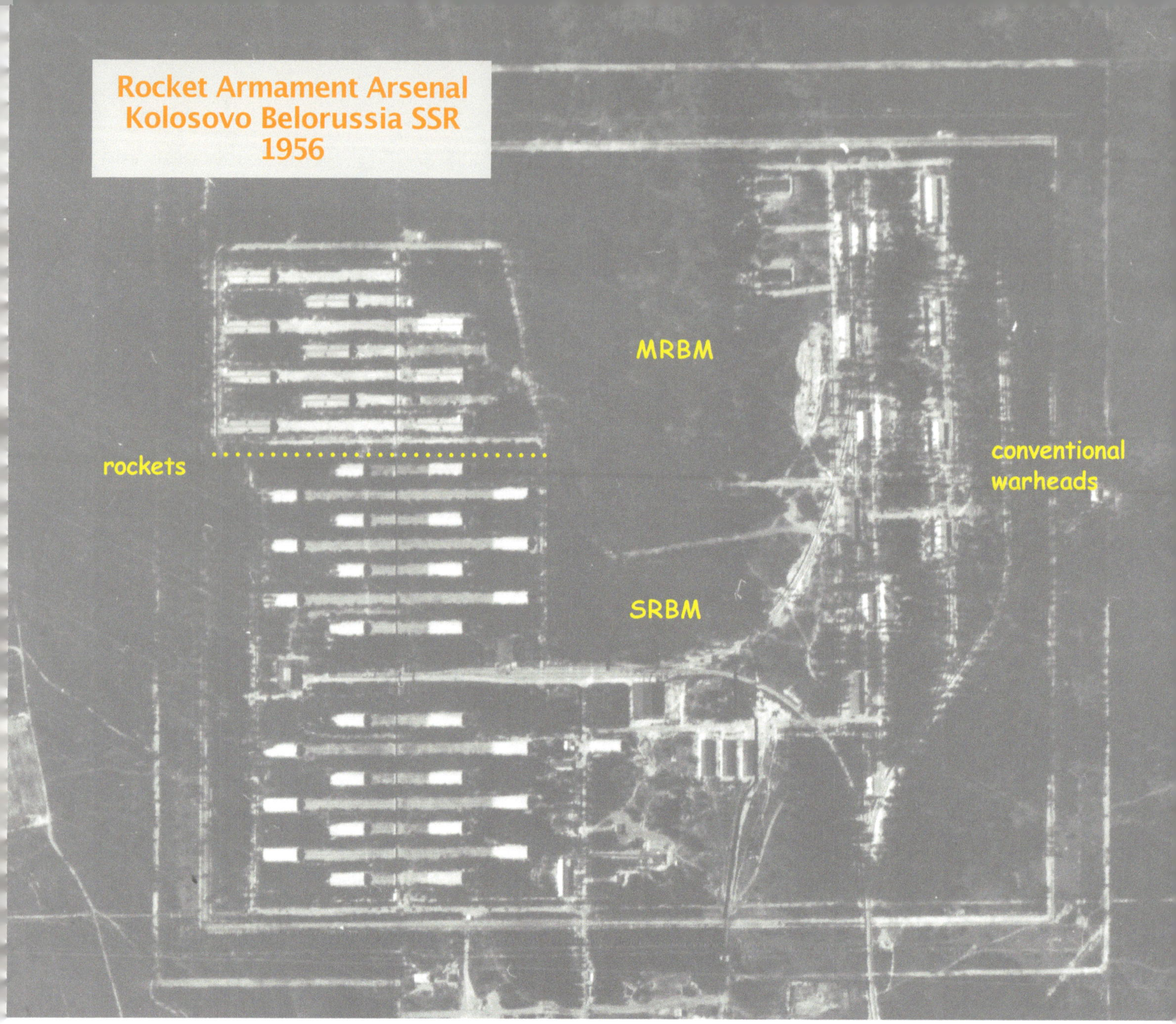

Rocket Armament Arsenal Kolosovo Belorussia SSR 1956

rockets

MRBM

SRBM

conventional warheads

satellite extensive geographic coverage, would launcher tallying become a Cold War intelligence fixture. Identification and tracking of RVSN and SV mobile rocket units, that replaced the deployable engineer brigades, would become reliable only in the 1970s with improved frequency and quality of signals and imagery collection. The opening of the Soviet émigré gates also provided valuable 'ground truth' from serving rocket unit personnel. The intelligence capabilities developed in this regard would be critical to verification of arms control treaties, beginning with the Intermediate Nuclear Force (INF).

The R-5M MRBM that had been successfully integrated into a deployable force of rocket units would constitute the most potent Soviet threat to European theater

targets until the first R-12 (SS-4 Sandal) MRBM un entered service from late 1959. The most extensi system and operational experience resided with Engineer Brigade, which would destine a leading ro in a breaking East-West melee.

The First Missile Crisis

Domestic US, and international, politics of the mid-late-1950s had been roiled by the 'ga controversies—the supposed Soviet superiority intercontinental bombers and missile technolog Calculated Soviet boasts and displays, notably by th star promoter Nikita Khrushchev, accentuated Weste fears. The first series of U-2 aircraft overflights of th USSR in 1956 essentially refuted the bomber ga

...tion, photographs revealing a minimal strategic ...rce at key airfields. The missile disparity issue could ...t be so easily resolved. The limited number of U-2 ...issions, and constricted geographic coverage of ...tential Soviet deployment areas, precluded any ...termination of the actual missile force level. Internal ...d external pressures on the Eisenhower ...ministration for counter-balancing action motivated ...itiatives to base IRBM on the periphery of the USSR. ...ependent on Strategic Air Command bombers as a ...clear deterrent until the Atlas ICBM became ...ailable in late 1959, the US viewed these missiles as ...eater weapons. To the Soviets any US nuclear ...stems that could target their territory constituted, by ...finition, a strategic issue.

...merican implementation of IRBM deployments ...nspired via two separate tracks; bilateral agreement ...ith Britain to base Thor, and through NATO, Jupiter in ...y receptive country. Presenting a basing proposal to ...e British Defence Minister in January 1957, ...reement in principle would be jointly announced on ...5 March at the Bermuda conference between ...esident Eisenhower and Prime Minister Macmillan. ...otional Soviet missile superiority seemed to receive ...unning confirmation with the 4 October successful ...biting of the Sputnik satellite. Further, a Moscow ...November parade in Red Square featured an ...pressive array of new MRBM and SRBM. ...hrushchev's missile boasts and threats now attained ...eater credence. A US offer of Jupiter missiles ...eadlined the NATO chiefs of government meeting in ...ris that December. Prolonged negotiations would ...isue to find hosts, and only in 1961 would Jupiter ...quadrons become operational in Italy and Turkey. ...onically, the Premier's theatrics boosting a rocket ...rce mirage instigated US and NATO theater missile ...eployment. Thor and Jupiter IRBM became a means, ...s much political as military, to restore the credibility ...f US technology and nuclear deterrent, while ...assuring Europeans of commitment to their defense. ...reality, the West had been responding to a perceived ...vith Soviet connivance) threat lacking any solid ...ntelligence substantiation—déjà vu! The Soviets

would then, in turn, embark on their own theater missile buildup.

Recently disclosed Russian information permits correlation of the sequence of missile deployment measures and counteraction. The Soviets quickly prepared to target the threat represented by the British Thor. A secret military survey group dispatched to East Germany sometime during early 1957 (possibly reacting directly to progress in the UK-US negotiations) selected installations near the towns of Vogelsang and Fürstenberg-Havel, 69 km and 83 km, respectively, north of Berlin. The only Soviet rocket capable of striking British Thor bases, the R-5M, could thus be sited within 860 km. Forward deployment offered the only Soviet option since any launch site in the Baltic region would be 180 km beyond maximum range. A formal UK-US Thor basing agreement had been signed on 22 February 1958, and construction of the launch complexes begun in May. The British work did not go unnoticed. On 24 May at a Warsaw Pact meeting in Moscow, Khrushchev issued a warning that rockets might be based in Central Europe as a countermove. He asked NATO leaders to "...not compel the Warsaw Treaty states to take reciprocal measures with regard to stationing rocket weapons."

A Soviet note proposing a European friendship pact, issued 15 July 1958, stated flatly that nuclear weapons and rocket sites had not been established outside of the USSR. This declaration only technically true however—physically weapons not present—Russian sources reveal that in early summer they had initiated a project to build rocket facilities at Vogelsang and Fürstenberg. By September, an agent of the Federal Republic's BND (*Bundesnachrichtendienst*) intelligence would report construction material for a rocket base in the vicinity. Reconnaissance aircraft in August-September, flying along one of the designated Berlin access corridors, had directed a 100-inch panoramic camera across terrain to the north. Photos taken revealed extensive construction under way at an installation known to NATO intelligence as Vogelsang 4823. Meanwhile, a US Air Force C-124 Globemaster delivered the first Thor missile to the premier British IRBM squadron at the Feltwell base on 19 September.

Energetic Soviet antimissile proselytizing in the first half of 1958 had later eased, unsurprisingly, since both sides already methodically progressed with respective programs for handling Thor. The Soviets renewed the peace campaign in the spring of 1959, and shifted against the still pending Jupiter bases. Diplomatic notes transmitted separately in April to the US and Italy warned of unspecified "security measures" to be taken. On 26 May Khrushchev, on tour in Tirana, threatened to place Soviet rockets in Albania as well as Bulgaria to counter Italian and Greek (then still under consideration) Jupiters; he and Defense Minister Malinovsky agreed that SRBM might be sufficient to target Italy. The prominence of Albania in bloc pronouncements would lead the CIA to schedule U-2 coverage in early 1959 to search for missile bases. The exchanges took place during a period of increasing tension over the status of Berlin. Khrushchev had announced in May a plan for an East German peace treaty that would terminate Western rights in the city.

The Soviets assigned the (presumed) mission of Thor hammerer to 72 Engineer Brigade. Russian information is conflicting but apparently elements of, or the entire, brigade moved from Medved to Kapustin Yar late in 1958. In what would become a well-worn path for Soviet rocket units, the brigade honed technical and operational skills at the maneuver grounds of the State Central Range. Training culminated with the live launching of eight R-5M. In January 1959 the brigade established a staging position near Gvardeysk in the, now, Kaliningrad enclave. Receiving orders for a "covert" deployment to the GDR, one of the brigade's three launch battalions remained at the base. This battalion may have occupied a permanent site that would later be identified on satellite photography near Gvardeysk. The 635 and 638 rocket battalions regrouped with their respective nuclear warhead handling units, as a test, via two different modes: one battalion by train, the other by air to Templin Airfield, located to the southeast of the deployment area. Each battalion brought two firing stands and six rockets.

The brigade arrival may have been noted by a BN agent who reported transports with "large bombs" January at Fürstenberg. The two bases apparently n fully complete at that time, MRBM nuclear warhea only delivered in mid-April and moved into, accordi to a Russian account, purpose-designed bunkers. period of unit training and familiarization probat followed until, early in May, the commander of Sov forces in the GDR reported directly to Khrushchev th 72 Engineer Brigade had achieved full operatior capability. Readiness at Vogelsang 4823 would confirmed that month by additional photographs tak by a corridor reconnaissance aircraft—three k structures now complete—and an identical s doubtless concurrently constructed, at a Fürstenbe casern designated 291. This installation, howev would not be seen on usable imagery until early 19 when acquired by the KH-4 satellite system. The Sov counter-punch had thus been mission-ready when t Royal Air Force 77 Squadron placed the first Briti Thor on alert the following month.

Minimal information on activities during t deployment is available, although brigade speciali likely conducted intensive rocket operations trainir Personnel of the MRBM brigade did not long enjoy t relative luxury of their East German base. Thr months after entering on combat duty, a withdraw order had been received. The Russian accounts stre a precipitous, hastily implemented move back Gvardeysk in August or August-September, surprisi officers and soldiers.

Did US and NATO intelligence services at the tir know that a Soviet missile brigade had deployed East Germany with Shyster MRBM? Well, sort temporarily. Matthias Uhl, in summarizing t episode, focused on BND agents reporting of Sov missile indications. Logically, such an informatic feed would betray the MRBM presence to the FRG a collaborators. This, however, is retrospecti spotlighting. The ongoing missile, and intensifyi Berlin, crises framed the contemporary intelligen picture. Images of an extensive Soviet missile thre d created a classic intelligence 'noise' environment, with a wave of sightings throughout the GDR identifying 'missile' bases and construction, movements of suggestive equipment by rail and road. The BND agent descriptions of Fürstenberg-Vogelsang area activity amounted to isolated drops in a flood of similar reports. A comparable atmosphere developed over an extended period prior to the October 1962 discovery of MRBMs in Cuba, but a post-assessment found that, of some 3500 agent and refugee 'missile' reports, eight had been valid.

US intelligence had been zeroing in on different evidence. On 9 September 1959 a shutterbug working the rail lines at Frankfurt-Oder, a major transshipment point for material entering or leaving the GDR, took photos of eight large trailers with tracked prime movers and other equipment on railcars. Sometime later, during attempts to identify the items, intelligence compared the trailers to those conveying missiles displayed at Moscow in 1957—bingo! The contemporary assessment identified the Frankfurt trailers to be the same as those on which Shyster MRBMs paraded through Red Square. A conclusion had been reached supposing a Shyster buildup under way—no intelligence analyst is likely to have suggested missiles in process of *withdrawal*—yet Russian information on the timeframe of 72 Engineer Brigade return to the USSR might correspond to the Frankfurt equipment. Rather odd that a retrograde transport would drop south more than 100 km when rail lines further north provide direct routes to Gvardeysk. There is, however, even a third scenario for the September rail sighting.

Additional evidence that evoked high interest involved observations of distinctive rail tank cars, which appeared to be venting the fumes of volatile liquid oxygen (LOX), the oxidizer used in the first generation of Soviet missiles. Intelligence assessments noted initial identification of the tank cars on East German rail lines beginning in late 1958. Particularly heavy movement had been noted, accounting for only those sightings considered most reliable, from April to August 1959, with the conclusion that direction of movement involving 75 of the 85 railcars seen clearly headed toward the Templin-Vogelsang area.

The Frankfurt MRBM photos, and apparent LOX railcars, had been appraised in the context of hundreds of human source reports of odd and missile-like objects. A 1961 intelligence summary of all the evidence concluded that Shyster had been stationed in the GDR and identified five potential deployment areas—four south of Berlin, and the fifth north, in the Templin Airfield-Vogelsang vicinity. Ranking two of the areas in the south "probable" the assessment included Templin-Vogelsang in a "possible" group. While considering the northern area as a potential launch zone, this assessment along with other reporting had been skewed by the tank railcar sightings to attribute an undefined logistical function. The mass of human source reporting lent higher credence to the southern options. The scale of evidence had led a late 1960 US guided missile intelligence working group to find "unanimously" that up to 200 Shyster missiles had been scattered throughout the GDR. The complement brought by 72 Engineer Brigade in 1959 had, of course, amounted to 12 rockets and four launchers.

Missing from the intelligence assessments is any awareness of the 1958 and May 1959 photos of Vogelsang 4823. Indicative structures had been built that formed part of the basis for the 1980 identification of MRBM at both Vogelsang and Fürstenberg 291. One type imaged clearly appeared to be an earth-mounded, concrete arch, bunker nearly as long as an American football field. The Soviets became the Bunker Kings of the Cold War. Implementing a doctrinal imperative to protect critical assets against a surprise nuclear strike, from the early 1950s they constructed, on an ever increasing scale, a wide variety of centrally designed, standardized hardened shelters for command and control facilities, WMD and delivery systems. Ironically, this strategy, despite the almost paranoid Soviet penchant for secrecy, exposed analytic opportunities to an opposing intelligence service heavily dependent on overhead pictures. Those versed in the esoteric art of bunkerology could derive far-reaching conclusions regarding planning, even intentions—when correctly related to operational concepts and organization. Unfortunately, opportunities abounded for misconnection as well.

The bunkers imaged at Vogelsang, and later at Fürstenberg, purposed identical to about 75 others in the first generation of MRBM nuclear warhead storage facilities—designated Class A and Class B by US intelligence—constructed at launch sites within the USSR. These bunkers stored and maintained warheads, and readied for mating to rockets at their firing pads. A second key structure (Soviet *objekt* 47) functioned as a rocket ready building with three long internal bays, and an annex at one end. Each of the East German caserns had one, slightly longer, version of similarly configured buildings built in large numbers for MRBM storage at four of the 1950s rocket armament arsenals. Some individual examples also could be identified in the USSR at early MRBM deployment areas—including one at an installation near Gvardeysk which, quite likely, operated as the staging base for 72 Engineer Brigade. As far as I could determine, these ready buildings related uniquely with MRBM. At least nine rocket bodies on transporters could be kept in each building. A third shelter (*objekt* 50) served as a launch equipment and vehicle ready building with four long bays. The Soviets erected structures of this type at the rocket armament arsenals, the Gvardeysk installation, and other missile-related facilities. The building, however, did not function exclusively for rocket equipment storage.

The functions of the trio might, separately, be subject to debate, but as a set the nuclear missile association is manifest. In the intell biz the obvious is not always apparent. Intelligence analysts in the period 1959 to mid-1961 would, if they had noticed the Vogelsang bunker on corridor photography, have had no reference points to identify purpose. Subsequently, as permanent MRBM launch sites and the attendant warhead areas continued to be identified on satellite

imagery within the USSR, the matches multipli Even in later reporting on the two East Germ installations, however, although remarking on t correspondence to MRBM nuclear warhead bunke no firm association would ever be made. The rock ready building is another matter: ten examples exist at the Kolosovo (Novaya Mezinovka) arsenal wh imaged in 1956, although the installation functi would not actually be understood until the 1960s. N connection to the other evidence pointing at t Vogelsang-Templin area had been achieved.

US intelligence assessments at all levels during 19. to 1961 attest the suspected Shyster presence. In a Joi Chiefs of Staff presentation before a Hou Appropriations subcommittee in January 196 General Nathan Twining stated that "indication existed for Shyster in East Germany. Natior Intelligence Estimate 11-4-60, issued in Decemb 1960, in a review of Soviet MRBM refers to "eviden that 700 n.m. [Shyster] missiles have been deployed East Germany…" The intelligence working group th found 200 of the missiles, while noting a lack of ha evidence, assumed a buildup from late 1958 throu; the fall of 1960. A July 1961 guided missile order battle document locates SS-3 in East Germany, wi the Templin area serving as a logistics base.

A September 1961 National Intelligence Estimate c ballistic missile strength and deployment, howeve delimits MRBM deployment to the USSR. Notably, t September 1962 Special Estimate regarding Cul predicates that external MRBM deployment had nev occurred. Declassified documents from the mont leading to, and during, the Cuban crisis show no hi of East German MRBM. Conclusions regarding Shyst forward deployment apparently vanished by late 196 The GDR Shyster story then became susceptible to th all too frequent, intelligence phenomenon of dropou the loss of institutional memory. I am thorough familiar with classified documents and discussions c WMD and missiles from the 1960s through the ear 1990s; no awareness whatsoever occurred regardir any MRBM deployment in East Germany. The la

Kolosovo MRBM rocket shelters

MRBM Base Vogelsang
East Germany
October 1965

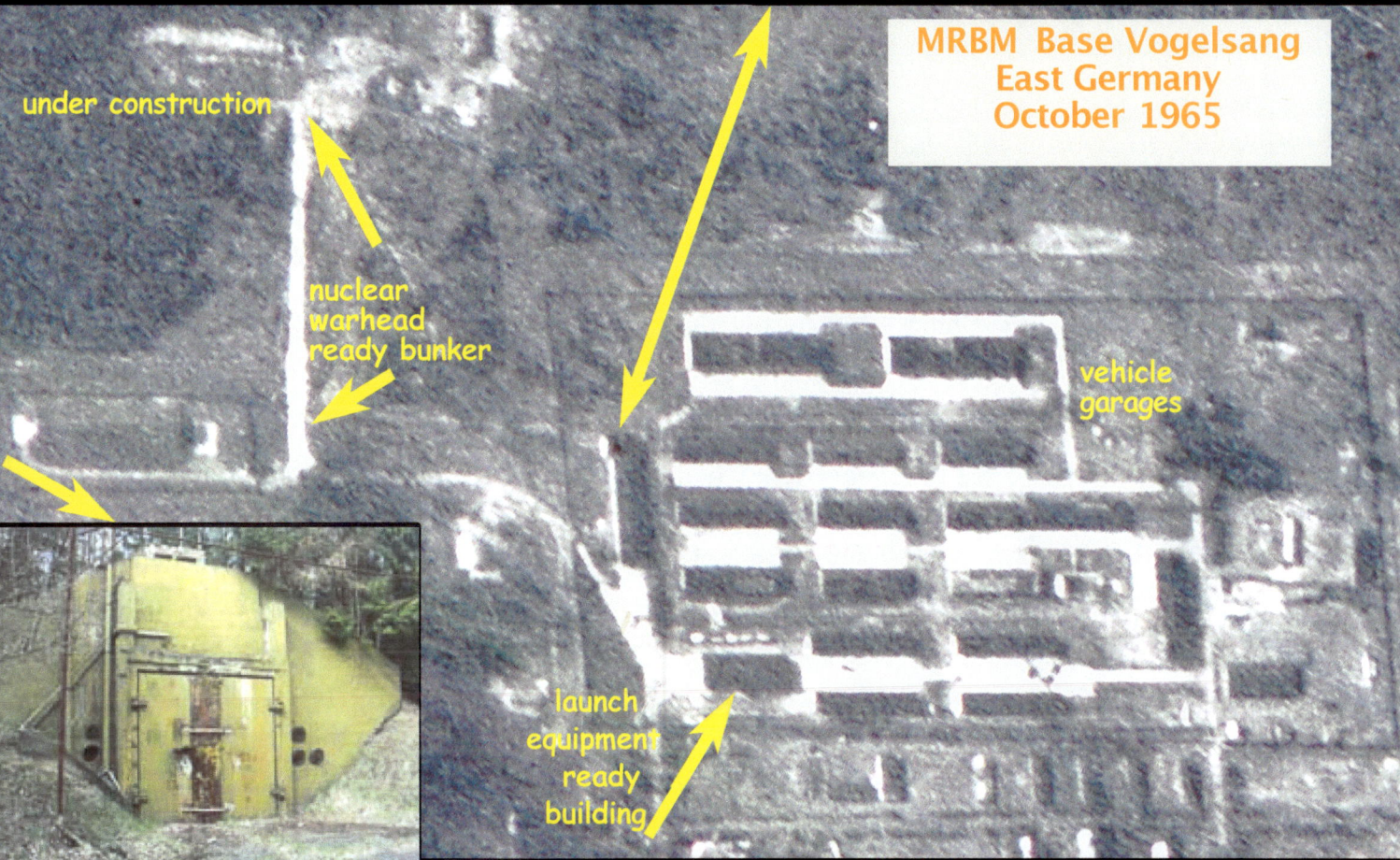

under construction

nuclear
warhead
ready bunker

vehicle
garages

launch
equipment
ready
building

R-5M Permanent BSP
Mukacevo Ukraine SSR

rocket
erector

system study of the SS-3, published in 1966, proclaimed that no evidence existed of the missile having been deployed outside of the USSR. My 1980 interlocutors, with years of experience in their respective Soviet groups of forces and strategic missile specialties, knew nothing concerning the Shyster episode. I only discovered the earlier reporting some years later, while researching another issue involving WMD in Central Europe, and additional material during preparation of this monograph.

Disappearance of the Shyster forward basing assessment may have resulted from a lack of reinforcing evidence. More telling, analysts likely misconstrued information from one of the Cold War's most valuable human intelligence sources, Oleg Penkovsky. It cannot be coincidental that he became an active agent during 1961. He has been attributed a key role in appraising the US of missile and Cuban developments but, paradoxically, may also have caused conclusions regarding Shyster to be abandoned. In the spring of 1961 Penkovsky had reported how Khrushchev had been deliberately magnifying the dimensions of the actual Soviet rocket force. Further, he stated that only four rocket brigades had been deployed with Soviet forces stationed in the GDR, backdating to 1959-1960. US intelligence assumed that these brigades fielded SRBM, including the liquid propellant SS-1b Scud A (R-11), and the FROG series (R-30)—and connected the extensive 1959 activity with initial deployment of these systems.

Russian disclosures on this phase of GDR MRBM deployment terminate with the 72 Engineer Brigade August/September 1959 return to Gvardeysk. In 1980 this retrograding had been invisible. In fact, intelligence indicators pointed to, not an ending, but rather continuity of MRBM in East Germany well into the 1960s, and a sequel not yet revealed by th Russians. Penkovsky had some relevant comments. Th transcript of the audio recording of his first Londo meeting with his intelligence contacts has bee declassified. Penkovsky refers to the four Soviet rock brigades in the GDR, but makes an emphat distinction. Varentsov (Marshal Sergey S. Varentsov, th SV Commander of Rocket-Artillery Troops) controlle part of the deployed rockets, but others actually ha subordination to Moskalenko (Marshal Kirill Moskalenko, RVSN Commander). To attentive listene or readers, it should have been unmistakable that, i April 1961, an RVSN rocket brigade continue deployment in East Germany.

Withdrawal—Or Replacement?

One Russian account informs that, upon withdrawal t Gvardeysk, the Soviets rearmed 72 Engineer Brigad with the new 2000 km R-12 MRBM. In 1960 the tapped brigade cadre experience by reorganizing as rocket division controlling R-12 regiments. Intelligenc reporting had posited Sandal operational in late 195 or early 1959. Russian sources mark 4 March 195 acceptance for service with the first units forming i May. As R-12 deployment preparations accelerated RVGK, and all future long range rocket units, receive a new overlord—the RVSN, created by a 17 Decembe 1959 decree of the Council of Ministers. Wha followed amounted to a wartime mobilization, usin classic Soviet force expansion methods. Decembe 1959 U-2 photography of the Kapustin Yar rang revealed Sandal equipment and system conversio training under way. Mainly through conversion c existing aviation and SV artillery units by 1 July 196 (according to the Russian web site rvsn.info) fifty-on R-12 rocket regiments had been created, eac accorded eight launchers—but only 94 of the nomina

08 on hand. Impending activation of the US Jupiter BM bases in Italy and Turkey, operational in 1961, at ast partly motivated this crash buildup. Soviet assified military writings of the period, however, dicate a wider target set embodied in a new onception of intense theater nuclear operations. The assive, rapid MRBM force expansion required an tensive period of assimilation—troop miliarization, technical and operational training— at must have strained military personnel and ganizational capabilities.

SSR-based R-12 now had British Thor, as well as the alian and Turkish Jupiter, in missile sights. Range is ot the only targeting consideration, however, since stance equates to ballistic flight time, an essential ctor in the deadly calculus of preemption. The soft-ted Thor on alert required about 15 minutes to ecute a launch sequence, defining a preemptive indow. Missiles can be designed to parameters ermitting a depressed trajectory that significantly duces flight time, but the tradeoff is substantial range irtailment. R-12 based in the western USSR did not ave the requisite range to strike British Thor quadrons, minimizing warning, with depressed ajectories. R-12 forward deployed, say in East ermany, would not only have flight times reduced early in half, but also the opportunity to conduct epressed trajectory strikes. In addition, new targets ad emerged. US Strategic Air Command bases in lorocco, used for B-47 bombers on alert rotation, quired a new landlord, urged out by the national overnment. In late 1959 SAC initiated a re-basing lan, developing three airfields in Spain. One of these, the south, would be out of Soviet rocket range for ore than two years. The other two could be struck by e R-12, but not from western USSR sites. The SAC

base near Zaragoza was well within, and Torrejón airfield near Madrid just within, range of forward deployed R-12. The Soviet capability to strike these and remaining theater targets from within the USSR would only be fulfilled with the introduction, beginning in early 1962, of the R-14 (SS-5 Skean) IRBM.

A BND agent reported that, on 10 September 1959, a new unit had arrived at Fürstenberg with personnel wearing artillery insignia, as did the previous tenant. This, on the day following the transit of MRBM equipment on railcars at Frankfurt. If 72 Engineer Brigade withdrew in August, as stated by a senior RVSN officer in the 1996 article, then those missile trailers could not have been the same R-5M. Intelligence identification as Shyster had been based on Moscow 1957 but the Sandal trailer only modified the Shyster version to handle greater weight; detailed photographs of Sandal support equipment only acquired later in Cuba. I have not succeeded in locating the Frankfurt photos to verify the system involved. A colleague, after reading the 1980 report, told me that he recalled photos of a Frankfurt rail sighting involving MRBM transporters accompanied by distinctive Sandal oxidizer and fuel tankers. Someone may have pulled the Frankfurt photos in late 1962, and recognized Sandal equipment from the Cuban sites. Penkovsky provided the identities of three of the four commanders of Soviet rocket brigades in the GDR. It is perhaps germane that two ranked colonels, commanding brigades explicitly said to be SV subordinate, one based at Weissenfels. *General mayor* Vinogradov, leader of the unspecified third brigade and another unnamed general, tellingly, outranked. If still around, it would be interesting to see an account by one of the generals concerning his tour

in East Germany.

Specific intelligence indications reinforce the other evidence to identify the new tenant at Fürstenberg 291 and at Vogelsang 4823—an R-12 rocket brigade. No such conclusion appears in any contemporary US intelligence reporting. In this scenario, the reason for the hurried evacuation of 72 Engineer Brigade becomes apparent: to reduce the interval in which priority theater targets lacked preemptive coverage. The R-5M deployment may have been a stopgap measure until R-12 rockets had been accepted in service. The Soviets had the options of expending months constructing new bases, or implementing a quick turnaround at existing bases, introducing a substantially more capable system.

Combat launch positions. Transportable metal launch stands erected and fired the R-5M and R-12 MRBM—but these systems could not be designated mobile—a crucial distinction. A mobile missile is transported and launched from the same self-propelled platform, in intelligence jargon a TEL (transporter-erector-launcher). Prior to the Cuban crisis, Penkovsky transmitted articles from a classified Soviet rocket troops journal that provided extensive information on R-12 launch operations, and nuclear warhead handling, along with technical and operational information on several rockets. These articles summarized experience, exercises, and problems encountered, during the R-12 'mobilization' including launch preparation timelines, and operations when a permanent site had not yet been constructed. The Soviets termed each missile firing site a BSP (*boevaya startovaya pozitsiya*) or combat launch position—— BSP established as permanent, field, and reserve sites. The classified material indicated that field BSP, prepared in advance, operated integral to R-12 deployment, this confirmed in much detail in later years by émigré reporting. When locating permanent MRBM sites in the USSR on satellite photography during the early 1960s, nearly 100 field BSP had also been identified, 5 to 30 km distant. The Soviets planned initial firings from the permanent BSP

followed by immediate road march relocation to field BSP to conduct supplemental launches.

Intelligence analysts had a grandstand view of R- equipment and operations in October 1962 when t Soviets shipped three regiments to Cuba. The SS-4 sit discovered on U-2 reconnaissance photograp actually constituted field BSP. Khrushchev exploit the transportability of R-12 to accomplish a politic fait accompli, by a rapid buildup of MRBM whi could establish firing positions in short timefram R-12 personnel had carried out the longest fie deployment in system history—over 9000 km! T Soviet dispatch of regiments rather than mo independently operating brigades, however, direct indicated the intention to construct permanent base Had the launch sites remained undiscovered, th would doubtless have been developed into a compl of permanent and field BSP as in the USSR. The tv R-14 IRBM regiments, turned back during the L blockade, could only operate from permanent BSP th required extensive infrastructure development.

MRBM operational procedures bear directly upon t East German deployment. Fürstenberg 291 ar Vogelsang 4823 functioned as garrisons, not BS lacking indications of firing positions within th installations. Area photography examined in 198 revealed, located about 8 km from each garrison, ar from each other, two characteristic field BSP. The thr key shelters at each installation had been arranged quickly assemble a convoy of rocket and warhe transporters, launch stands, erectors, propella tankers, and other support vehicles for a road march the field BSP. Rockets could be ready to fire about s hours after receipt of a displacement order. Two fie BSP conformed exactly to the MRBM two-battalic organization of the early 1960s, seen within the USS and in Cuba. Each BSP had four grouped, separate clearings for battalion launch stands. High resolutic imagery, still classified, revealed standard elongate concrete aprons, even cable traces. The clearing aprons at the BSP generally aligned on the sam azimuth, with about ten degrees difference betwee

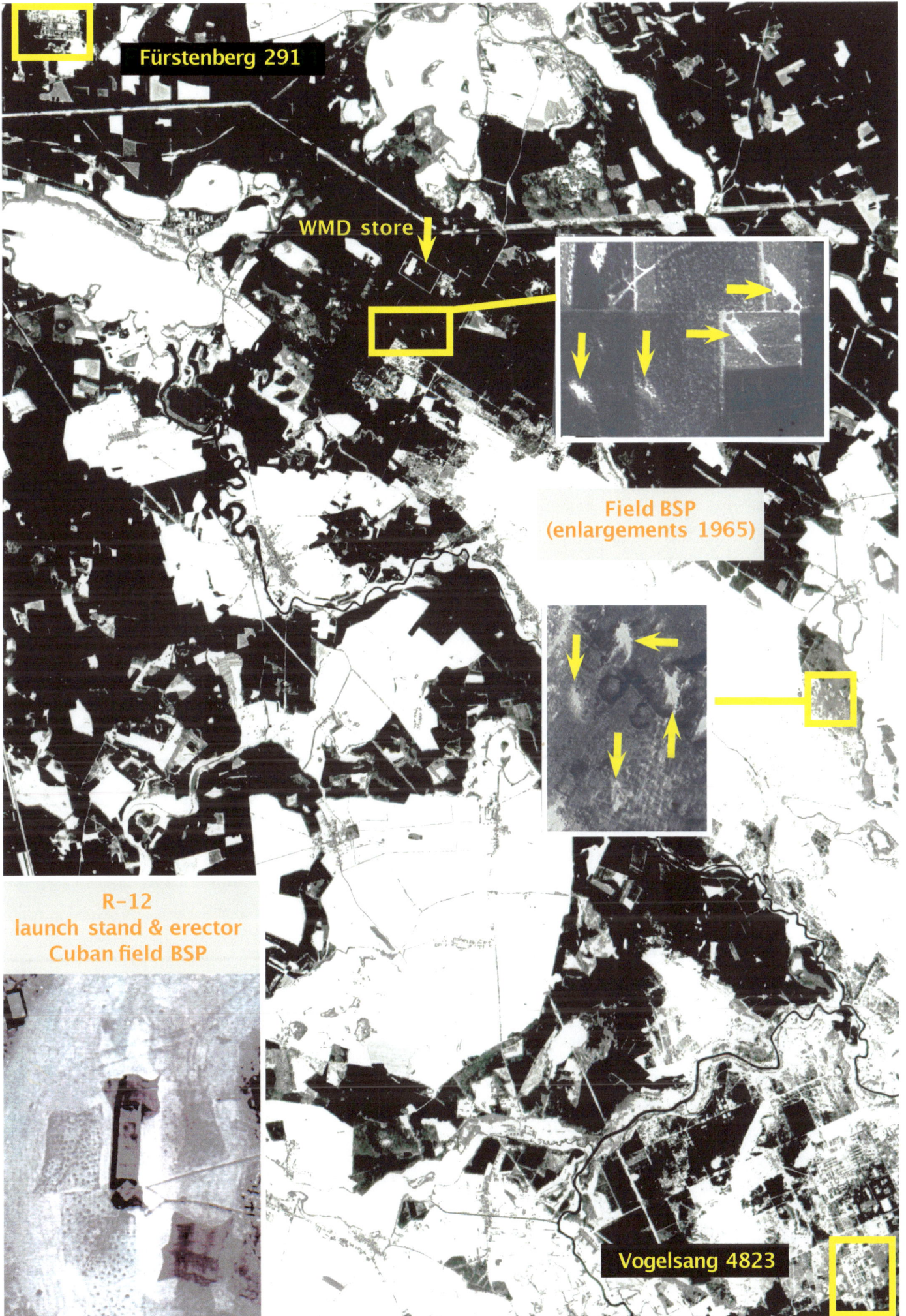

Fürstenberg 291

WMD store

Field BSP
(enlargements 1965)

R−12
launch stand & erector
Cuban field BSP

Vogelsang 4823

the two groupings. Single characteristic R-5M launch pads would later be found by ground survey near each of the garrisons; likely training positions since BSP would have been dispersed.

These field BSP, which are first discernible, on KH-4 satellite photography of September 1962—cleared sometime after 1956—are problematic for Shyster. The Russian accounts of the 72 Engineer Brigade deployment specify that two battalions moved, with two launch stands per battalion. Each field BSP, however, has twice that number of clearings, equating to the battalion configuration of contemporary R-12 deployments. An 'archaeological' ground survey of these clearings revealed obvious remains including cast-in-place concrete platforms; with firing stand placement indicated by a circular arrangement of reinforcing blocks and eight 'bow tie' metal keyways. Concrete and metal cable conduits extend to adjacent launch control revetments. Six of the platforms are square pads, while two are aprons about 50 meters in length. Russian information refers to a 4 April 1959 Ministry of Defense Directive to reorganize battalions as regiments with four launchers; each of those in the GDR by the first half of May attained combat duty status with four R-5M firing stands.

Zakharov's R-12. Matthias Uhl later rummaged files at the Russian State Archive of Socio-Political History, finding an item regarding an 18 December 1959 report by Marshal M. V. Zakharov—Commander of the Soviet Group of Forces, Germany. Zakharov stated "that maintaining an R-12 brigade in the GDR, excluding equipment and technology, cost 8.1 million rubles…" Some three months after the supposed ending of MRBM deployment outside of the USSR the head of Soviet troops in East Germany remained concerned with operating the replacement missile system.

Military unit 18300. In October 1961 an assessment, using the military unit methodology, discussed two entities that had been noted conducting long range missile firings in the last half of 1959 at a range

associated with Kapustin Yar. One unit had later be located at an MRBM site in the Baltic region. T second numeric had been noted again three da earlier in a context suggestive of a Soviet military u stationed in the GDR. These connections led t analyst(s) to conclude that a Soviet MRBM associat unit had been based outside the USSR, probably East Germany. Apparently not a popular conclusion the sentence had been lined out in the message—k remained legible. Usual practice would indicate th there had been a follow-up instruction to recipients delete the sentence, just as a judge might tell a jury disregard testimony they have just heard.

These unit numbers most often would be randon bestowed. But documented instances had be observed by intelligence of block assignments, sequence given to newly established units a installations. Russian information (particularly rvs info) and Cold War intelligence enables an interesti assemblage connected to those first 51 R regiments.

- 18279—85 RP (Rocket Regiment) formed Decemb 1958; Kapustin Yar training completed 5 Augu 1959 after rearming with R-12.

- 18282—115 RP formed August 1958 armed wi R-5M; stationed Latvia SSR; by July 1966 rearm with new R-900 *Temp S* (SS-12 Scaleboard).

- 18291—94 RP formed September 1958 but n placed on combat duty with R-12 until mid 1960.

- **18300**

- 18301

- 18302

- 18303—132 RP formed October 1958 in Far Ea armed/rearmed R-12 uncertain date; 1966 rearm with R-900; declared INF Treaty at Novosysoyevka

- 18304

- 18305

18306

18307—264 PRTB (nuclear warhead custodian) supporting 115 RP

18308

18309—267 PRTB supporting 132 RP

...tending the R-12 deployment:

18323—109 RP formed in December 1958; R-12 combat duty in 1961

18376—151 RP formed in May 1959; later armed with R-12

...randomly assigned, there would be no import; but a ...ock assignment of any part of this sequence would ...dicate that unit 18300 had been among or the first...

...arheads for Vogelsang.

In mid-1964, a requirement ...r additional nuclear warheads is evident at the ...ogelsang base. A second MRBM warhead ready ...unker, identical to the predecessor, would be ...onstructed over the next year-and-a-half. Obviously ...ome development regarding the occupant made it ...ecessary to essentially double storage capacity. There ...no direct evidence of motivation. Within the USSR, ...om early 1964, some R-12 regiments had been ...ugmented with third battalions to provide a silo ...unch capability using the new R-12U rocket variant. ...similar expansion may have been implemented in a ...DR brigade to increase the initial salvo fire. However ...o third field BSP can be identified in the immediate ...irstenberg-Vogelsang area. While bunker two ...ontinued in work, March 1965 imagery captured ...ogelsang a few days after a moderate snowfall— ...ence the cover replication. Extensive melting due to ...ehicle movement had occurred at garages with about ...0 percent of the 230 standard truck capacity. More ...gnificantly, similar disturbance had taken place on ...e road to bunker one, within the secured compound, ...nd at both bunker entrances. Unless the local ...ommander had taken to stocking his German beer ...side a nuclear warhead bunker, the leading ...xplanation for the high level of activity evident must be the continued presence of kegs containing a decidedly lethal brew. Occupancy considerations are complicated by the later identification of an SV nuclear-technical unit supporting 2 Guards Tank Army, transition date uncertain.

Operation *Tuman*. A 1999 issue of the Russian military journal *Krasnaya Zvezda* conveyed in an article entitled "The Order That Never Came" the recollections of retired Colonel Vladimir Aleksandrov concerning Operation Fog. Aleksandrov had been appointed commander of an R-12 rocket regiment in 1961, newly formed at two existing regiments of 50 Rocket Army in Belorussia for a specific task— deployment to the Fürstenberg-Vogelsang area in the GDR. While shaping up the unit, Aleksandrov and six officers of the new regiment traveled in late September to the siting area, where they appraised facility conditions. The Colonel stated construction work had been conducted at two field positions designated BSP-1 and BSP-2. The group then returned to the regiment to continue combat preparation and await the movement order. After an anxious period, the Soviets cancelled the planned deployment; and the regiment would be disbanded the following year. Colonel Aleksandrov surmised that impending entry into service of the R-14 IRBM had overridden the need to forward base any R-12. This article is actually an extract from a memoir by Aleksandrov, found by Matthias Uhl, that provides additional details. Unit number 54310 represented the rocket regiment while the nuclear support outfit had been assigned 14276. Aleksandrov's memoir contains a description and diagram of the planned regimental disposition, but the latter inaccurately depicts the relative location of local towns. In addition, his statement of BSP directions-distances from Fürstenberg and Vogelsang does not correspond to the known BSPs, while buildings and other elements said to have been constructed are not visible even on early satellite imagery.

A superficial reading of his account might explain post-1959 activity in the Fürstenberg-Vogelsang area,

Germany
R–12

cables
conduit

pad with firing table keyways

firing apron

cables >
conduit

<junction box

launch control revetment

Taurage
Lithuania
R–12

Paplaka
Latvia
R–5M

particularly at the BSPs. Unfortunately for a tidy history, there are more significant problems:

- Marshal Zakharov had placed R-12 in the GDR in December 1959

- Penkovsky had identified an RVSN rocket brigade in the GDR five months earlier than Aleksandrov

- Vogelsang's second MRBM warhead bunker building away three years after his departure, along with continued high level of activity

- the October 1961 information, although acquired during the period Aleksandrov visited East Germany, involved a different rocket unit in existence since at least 1959

- MRBM transporters at Frankfurt in September 1959, that may not have been R-5M

Seven of the eight concrete platforms in Germany survived (at least until I pinpointed these in 2004), including metal keyways for bolting firing tables. With a minimum of refurbishment, they would have been ready for the next salvo. These pads indisputably had been purposed for the R-12 system. Both R-5M and R-12 launch pads are now accessible in their Baltic deployment areas. The keyways at all seven German pads are identical to those of one of the Baltic systems—the R-12. Pending Russian clarifications, Colonel Aleksandrov's activities, and evidence currently available, suggest a provisional unit rotation, an additional, rather than an initial, R-12 deployment, or even forward movement during 1961 of more than one regiment.

Beginning in the spring of 1959, an ever-increasing collection of varied intelligence evidence had been pointing to MRBM at the Fürstenberg and Vogelsang installations. By 1964 all the pieces of the GDR missile puzzle now known had become available—imagery of indicative structures and field BSP; extensive knowledge of Soviet MRBM basing practice and operational procedures; the 1959 tank railcar sightings, highlighting the significance of the Vogelsang-Templin area; unit tracking; agent reporting;

and the Frankfurt equipment photography. An Penkovsky had provided a solution. Importa subsequent evidence emerged in accounts by t operators spelling out precisely what had be occurring. A Soviet Sandal brigade may still ha present in East Germany into the mid-1960s, posing preemptive threat to key NATO assets. Instea connections would not be made until 16 years later

The, presumable, withdrawal of the GDR R-12 is invisible as in the R-5M situation. The extensi preparations necessary for MRBM basing have fe parallels in a retrograde movement. My 1980 rep posited a pullout during the mid-1960s, based highly circumstantial evidence, and nothing mc substantial has since emerged. Soviet deployment the R-14 IRBM, starting early in 1962, had gradua closed any European theater range gap. The target that the MRBM may have been assigned had begun dissipate during 1963. Stand down of the British Th IRBM began in November 1962, and completed September 1963. Rotational alert basing of SAC B- at Spanish airfields had been terminated in April 196 and the bomber replaced entirely by the B-52. T second warhead bunker at Vogelsang, however, h probably been mounded by late 1965, providing t key indicator of continued MRBM occupation.

US intelligence concluded, and Russian informati confirms, that the remaining Soviet R-5M invento had been phased out during 1966 to 1967. In additio the Soviets initiated during the same period, substantial if gradual, reduction of R-12 deployed both the Western and Far East USSR. The cleare indication that any GDR Sandal may have participat in the reduction occurred in the spring of 1967, wi the start of construction on a WMD storage facility ju 800 meters from the northern field BSP. A doze identical facilities had been built in Central ar Eastern Europe during 1966 to 1969 holding Sovie controlled WMD stocks intended for release Warsaw Pact allies during a war with NAT Seemingly unlikely that the BSP would continue operational use with an especially sensiti

stallation nearby. Other, more subtle, physical
anges at both garrisons beginning in late 1965 might
so point to vacation. My WAG (an oft-used
telligence technical term) then and now spotlights
066 as the pivotal year—which also pertains to the
ewly fielded R-900 *Temp-S*. During 1966-67 at least
e R-12 and four R-5M regiments rearmed with, or
ntributed to, R-900 brigades—whether unit 18300
ad also been involved cannot yet be documented.
st Germany may have seen the last deployed MRBM
it Fürstenberg and Vogelsang would, in the not
stant future, replay their basing roles in a new theater
issile counterpoise.

Missile Crisis Reprise

e apparition of theater nuclear missiles,
ke a virus that remains dormant for a
hile and then reappears, developed into
leading European security issue of the
te 1970s into the 1980s. The US and
ATO felt impelled to respond to another
issile gap but this occurrence had a
lid evidentiary basis. During the second
alf of the 1970s the Soviets began to
igment, and replace elements of, the
960s R-12 MRBM and R-14 IRBM force
y an extensive deployment of the *Pioner*
S-20 Saber) mobile IRBM. *Pioner*
ebuted one of the most impressive
eapons fielded by either side during the Cold War. A
stemic innovation with multiple warheads, a new
e of mobile vehicles, permanent BSP, and distinctive
eld operations, the scale of the Soviet threat could not
e ignored. In December 1979 the NATO Council
pproved European deployment by the US of 108
GM-31C Pershing II 1770 km IRBM launchers, and
64 BGM-109G Gryphon 2500 km cruise missiles to
atch the Soviet buildup. This decision touched off a
idespread 'peace' campaign against deployment,
heered on and reinforced by Soviet gambits that
ersisted strongly reminiscent of the 1950s missile
risis.

Soviet propaganda, such as in *The Threat to Europe*
series, claimed that their early rocket deployments had
been motivated by US forward based systems, and that
Pioner represented only an modernization of
equilibrium maintenance. This convenient equation
belied by those Soviet classified writings of the early
1960s that defined a substantially wider variety of
targets for strategic rockets in theater operations,
repeated openly in the editions of the opus *Military
Strategy*. Nonetheless, the Soviet mindset featured a
reciprocation imperative—any action by the other side
demanded a countermove. The instrument chosen to
demonstrate Soviet resolve entailed one
of the least known, and most poorly
understood, rocket systems.

US intelligence obtained insights into
early 1960s Soviet thinking regarding the
nature of theater nuclear warfare from the
classified journals provided by Oleg
Penkovsky. The first issues of a new top
secret edition of *Voyennaya Mysl'*
(Military Thought) contained articles by
generals offering a simplified solution for
operations against NATO—basically
lobbing nuclear multi-megatons with a
relatively small ground force to waltz in
and take over. One general did conclude
that destroying only about ten percent of
Western European residential geography would be
necessary. Other generals pointed out that, in this
scenario, the Soviet occupiers would encounter most
unpleasant conditions. Eventually the General Staff
shelved the Big Bang variant in favor of a more
balanced approach, in which nuclear rockets
remained the determining factor. A Soviet Front, the
operational-strategic formation for conducting theater
operations, had been projected to be capable of
advancing in Western Europe to a depth of 1000 to
1200 km at an average advance rate of 100 km every
24 hours. In early 1961 Marshal Varentsov argued in
detail why the SV required a rocket that could range
the full depth of this Front operation, his objective to

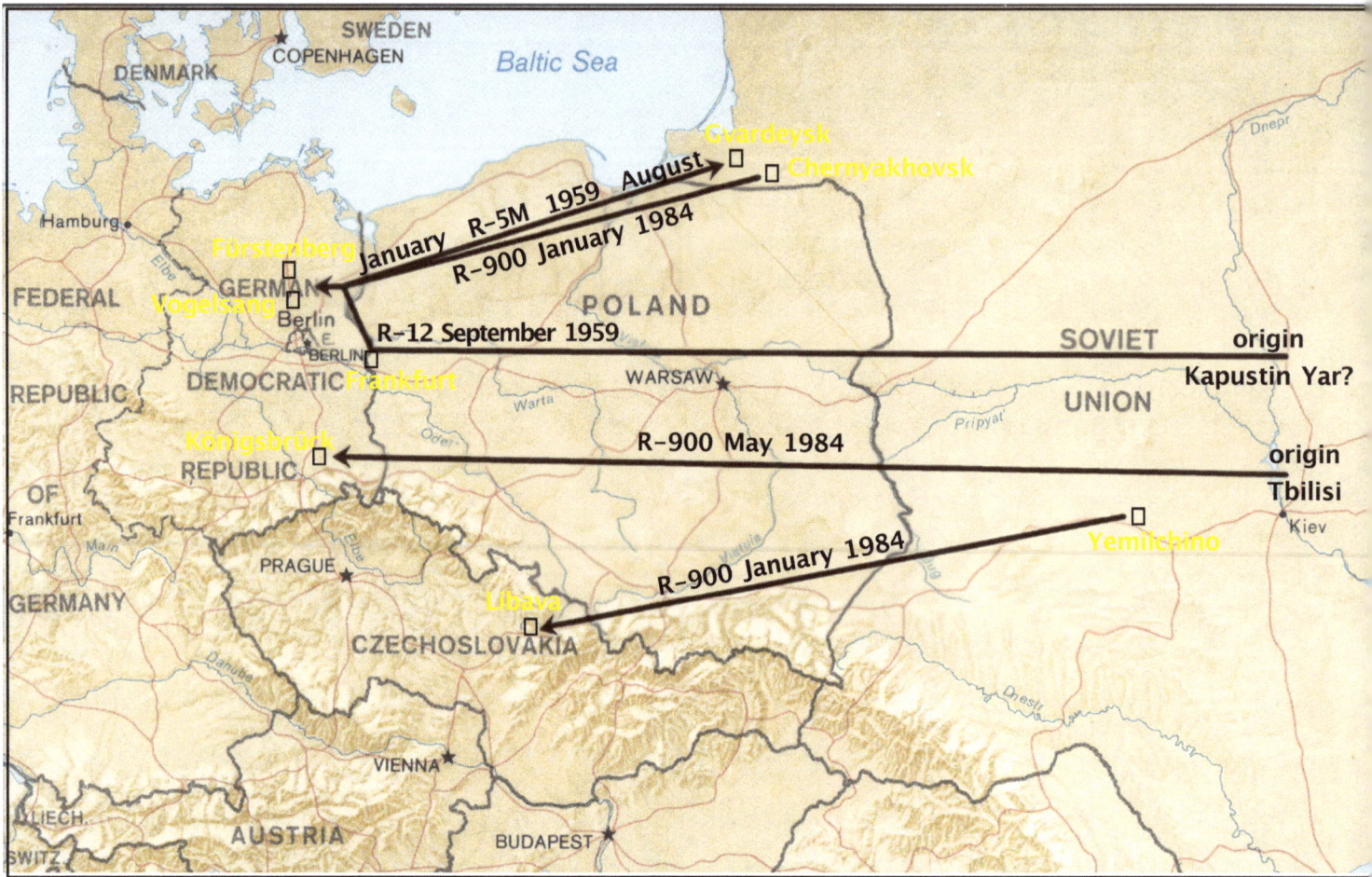

initiate a discussion of the issue. The R-5M, provided to the SV in 1959, met the range criterion, but system mobility had been poorly matched to the dynamic operations envisioned.

The "discussion" proceeded unbeknownst to US intelligence. The likely technical tasking formulated for the designers would be fulfilled within five years by the R-900 (Scaleboard) mobile rocket. The Soviet system nickname, *Temp* (rate or pace), directly reflected the conceptual theater mission. Although transported and fired from the same Maz-543 wheeled vehicle utilized by the SV R-300 (SS-1c Scud B) SRBM, the system featured a number of innovations. Unlike R-300, the two-stage rocket contained solid propellant, and could be transported longer distances on the launcher due to a protective pod enclosure. The US had some problems monitoring Scaleboard. Uncertainties regarding modifications to the original rocket, or even replacement with an entirely new design, resulted in designations that bounced about, from SS-12 to SS-12/22 to SS-22, then back as SS-12 Mods. At one point a new missile had been declared when an article

9M79 emerged, which seemed to sequence th original 9M76 designation. The 9M79 would turn o instead to represent the SS-21 Scarab SRBM.

The Soviets also had problems handling R-900. By th year of system acceptance for service the operation environment had radically altered. Partly due to th mutually reflective surfaces of Soviet and US-NAT nuclear doctrine, and probably more realist assessments by the deep thinkers of the General Sta by the mid-1960s the parameters of European theate warfare had become sharply constricted. A expectation that nuclear weapons would n necessarily be used at the outset of a campaign, or n at all, curtailed both anticipated rates of advance an depth nearly in half. The new R-900 outranged thes limits, and the 900 km nominal range approximate the 1,000 km breakpoint for strategic rockets. Littl evidence of the bureaucratic tussle that must hav ensued reached intelligence analysts; but as detecte system activity increased operational control evident had veered RVSN rather than part of the SV missi complement. RVSN subordination may have bee

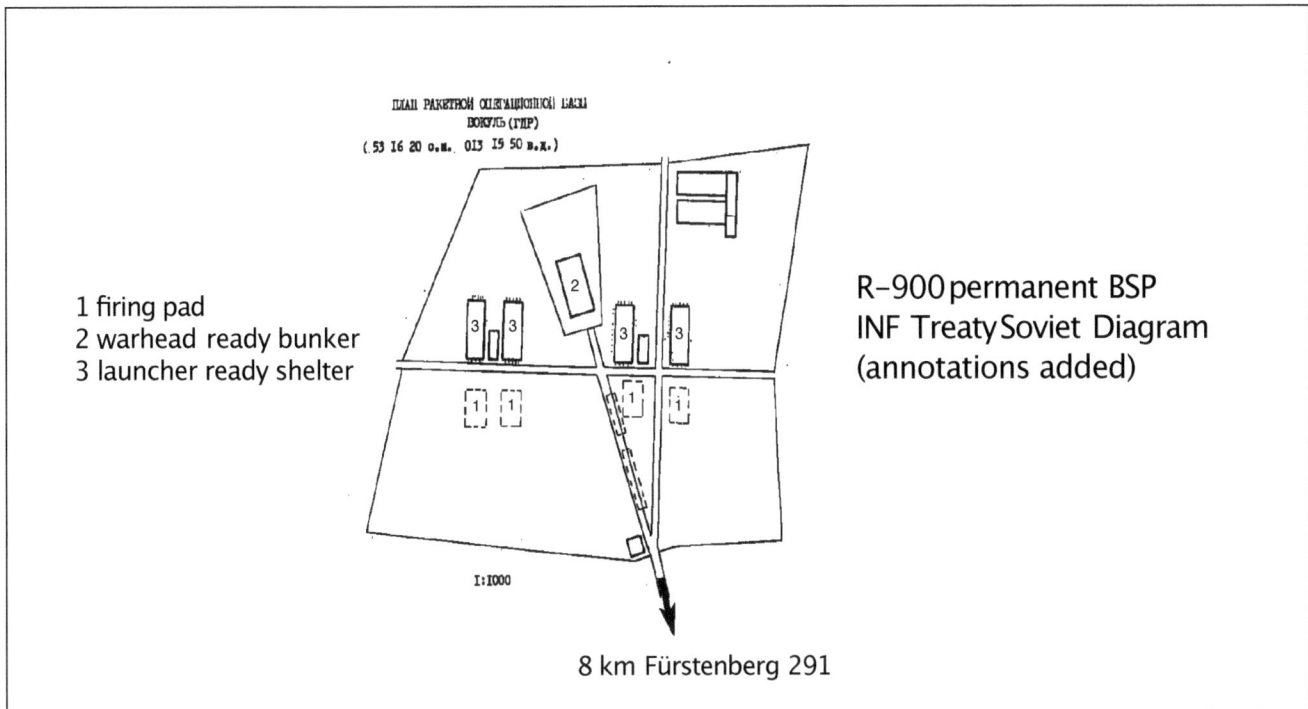

ПЛАН РАКЕТНОЙ ОПЕРАЦИОННОЙ БАЗЫ
ВОКУЛЬ (ГПР)
(53 16 20 о.ш. 013 15 50 в.д.)

1 firing pad
2 warhead ready bunker
3 launcher ready shelter

1:1000

R–900 permanent BSP
INF Treaty Soviet Diagram
(annotations added)

8 km Fürstenberg 291

nsolation, or an interim substitute, for the poor sults experienced with the first attempt to develop a obile IRBM. The earliest indications of deployment anifested in the spring of 1967, on imagery tection of launch position modifications at three RBM permanent BSP—all formerly Shyster—at vardeysk and Simferopol (Balki) in the Western SSR; and Manzovka (Kremovo) in the Far East. urther deployments on the Soviet border with China l occurred at deactivated IC-IR-MRBM sites.

/SN stewardship of the R-900, however, would be irtailed. Subsequent to 1970 signs of SV re- ibordination mounted. The deployed force omprised about ten brigades and independent ittalions by 1983. This R-900 mobile rocket force onstituted a tool readily capable, not only of an imediate Soviet riposte, but also paring retargeting ' the Soviet IR-MRBM force against the initial US iissile deployments. The system also provided an ition to conduct theater strikes with conventional recision weapons. An R-900 forward move to target 'S theater missiles presented, on a much larger scale, counterpart to the transference of 72 Engineer rigade against British Thor, attaining a similar reemptive posture. The stage would be set on 23 ovember 1983 with the walkout of the Soviet delegation from Geneva missile negotiations. The delivery of Pershing II to the US 56 Field Artillery Brigade in West Germany on 15 December may have been the tripwire for another Soviet rocket migration.

Unlike 1959, this deployment would be anything but covert. From late June through October 1983, the designated R-900 units openly parked in full view of US photo reconnaissance satellites, in battalion and brigade formations; for extended periods; in or near their home garrisons. This astonishing and unprecedented divergence from normal diligent surveillance avoidance security measures could only have been intended to direct a warning to the West of the consequences of US systems introduction. The 152 Rocket Brigade based at Chernyakhovsk, in the Kaliningrad region, participated in the display, and moved to the northern GDR. A brigade at Chernyakhovsk had been associated with the Gvardeysk 1967 BSP activity. The 122 Rocket Brigade moved in parallel from home base at Yemilchino in Ukraine to the Hranice-Libava area of Czechoslovakia, while the 119 Rocket Brigade followed four months later from a permanent garrison near Tbilisi in the Transcaucasus into southern East Germany.

In January 1984 the Soviets publicly announced the forward movement of "enhanced range" operational-tactical rockets, and in the third week US satellites imaged the first transferred Scaleboard equipment—at Fürstenberg 291 and Vogelsang 4823. During the 25th anniversary month of the arrival of 72 Engineer Brigade, the MRBM bases had again been occupied by rockets aimed at US theater systems. The Soviets thereby also re-affirmed the R-900 connection to the RVSN. As in the 1958 preparation of missile bases, the Soviets in the 1983 pre-deployment phase made identifiable alterations to existing garrisons, mainly for warhead storage. However additional bases had been built from scratch in the northern GDR, and Czechoslovakia, only after the brigades arrived, completed in the fall of 1984. The new installations demonstrated that the Soviets had been peeking at the bunkerology manual. A deliberate variation from standard structures had been implemented in the arrangement of the bases, and between deployment areas, as well as architecture of warhead and rocket hardened storage shelters. The stratagem would be successful for a short time—Scaleboard association of the new bases not immediately evident, and some intelligence analysts tried to connect them to unrelated scenarios. The basing pattern would be sorted out only by mid-1984.

US intelligence had detected signs of the Scaleboard brigade departures from their USSR garrisons, and arrival in East Europe, but not the actual transits. The Soviets managed to move more than 700 vehicles in one or two week transports—including many large Maz launchers and transporters, rockets, warheads,

mobile cranes, and specialized equipment—entir[e] unnoticed. The Soviets established during 19[ ] elaborated regional complexes of garrisons, logist[ic] bases, and permanent BSP for performing combat du[ty] Intell assessed the original number of launch[ers] deployed at 42; and some evidence existed [of] battalion organic reserve launchers that wo[uld] increase the total by nine. But the 1987 INF Treaty d[ata] exchange declared 58 launchers. The launch[er] complement may have been augmented to maintai[n] maximized alert capability—while also possible t[hat] the Soviets moved in more launch battalions th[an] assessed—but the excess likely formed train[ing] batteries. The R-900 deployment, unlike the earl[y] MRBM, would end in the glare of publicity and vid[eo] cameras in early 1988, withdrawn for complete syste[m] elimination under the terms of the INF Treaty.

From the intelligence perspective an order [of] magnitude improvement in analytical outcomes h[ad] transpired in the two decades between East Germ[an] missile moves. Assessments of the first deployme[nt] constituted a dismal failure while those of the 198[ ] rated at least a qualified success. The different[ce] inhered the substantial enhancement of collecti[on] tools, and the development of a solid knowledge b[ase] of Soviet missile operations. But errors of interpretati[on] abided in the perspective of analysts in the seco[nd] missile crisis despite the considerable extent [of] evidence available. Ultimately, intelligence proble[m] solving, regardless of the quality and quantity [of] information, resolves to the ability of analysts [to] recognize and put the pieces together, in the ri[ght] order.

Resources

Selected background readings, references, and other related material may be accessed at
<https://reality.rngend.com/>

R-12 regiment order of battle <https://rvsn.info/missiles/r_12_reg_01.html>

Matthias Uhl; *Krieg um Berlin?*; ISBN 978-3-486-58542-1; 2008; p106 Zakharov

Illustration Credits

R-5M launcher and R-12 trailer photographs; R-12 launcher drawing Publishing House, Arms and
Technologies,; Moscow.; *Russia's Arms and Technologies—The XXI Century Encyclopedia* VOL I
Strategic Nuclear Forces

Paplaka and Taurage photographs <http://www.flickr.com/photos/martintrolle/sets>

Author

Charles Tuten performed CIA analysis from 1972 through 1995. Specialties included Soviet and
Warsaw Pact WMD, missile systems, and theater operations. He also aided analysts grappling with
similar problems in other parts of the world. Current activities include consulting and writing on
intelligence issues.